The School of Life: The Meaning of Life

First published in 2019 by The School of Life
First published in the USA in 2020
This paperback edition published in 2025
930 High Road, London, N12 9RT
Authorised representative in the EEA: The School of Life Amsterdam,
Frederiksplein 54, 1017 XN Amsterdam, Netherlands

Copyright © The School of Life 2019

Cover design by @marciamihotichstudio
Printed and bound in Great Britain by by CPI Group (UK) Ltd,
Croydon, CR0 4YY

All rights reserved. This book is sold subject to the condition
that it shall not be resold, lent, hired out or otherwise circulated
without express prior consent of the publisher.
A proportion of this book has appeared online at
www.theschooloflife.com/articles

Every effort has been made to contact the copyright holders
of the material reproduced in this book. If any have been
inadvertently overlooked, the publisher will be pleased to make
restitution at the earliest opportunity.

The School of Life publishes a range of books on essential topics
in psychological and emotional life, including relationships,
parenting, friendship, careers and fulfilment. The aim is always
to help us to understand ourselves better – and thereby to grow
calmer, less confused and more purposeful. Discover our full
range of titles, including books for children, here:
www.theschooloflife.com/books

The School of Life also offers a comprehensive therapy service,
which complements, and draws upon, our published works:
www.theschooloflife.com/therapy

www.theschooloflife.com

ISBN 978-1-916753-33-4

10 9 8 7 6 5 4 3 2

The School of Life: The Meaning of Life

The true ingredients of fulfilment

The School of Life

Contents

	Introduction	7
1	Sources of Meaning	11
	i. Love	13
	ii. Family	21
	iii. Work	33
	iv. Friendship	51
	v. Culture	63
	vi. Politics	85
	vii. Nature	89
	viii. Philosophy	97
2	Obstacles to Meaning	101
	i. Vague self-understanding	103
	ii. Provincialism	105
	iii. Selflessness	108
	iv. Immortality	111
	v. The art of storytelling	112

Introduction

To wonder too openly, or intensely, about the meaning of life sounds like a peculiar, ill-fated and unintentionally comedic pastime. It isn't anything an ordinary mortal should be attempting, or would get very far by doing. A select few might be equipped to take on the task and discover the answer in their own lives, but such ambition isn't for most of us. Meaningful lives are for extraordinary people: saints, artists, scholars, scientists, doctors, activists, explorers, leaders ... If we ever did discover the meaning, it would, we suspect, be incomprehensible; perhaps written in Latin or in computer code. It wouldn't be anything that could orient or illuminate our activities. Without always acknowledging it, we are operating with a remarkably ungenerous perspective on the meaning of life.

Yet, in truth, the subject is for everyone. It is for all of us to wonder about, and define, a meaningful existence. There need be nothing forbidding about the issue. A meaningful life can be simple in structure, personal, usable, attractive and familiar. This is a guidebook to it.

A meaningful life is close to, but at points importantly different from, a happy life. Here are some of its ingredients:

- A meaningful life draws upon, and exercises, a range of our higher capacities; for example, those bound up with tenderness, care, connection, self-understanding, sympathy, intelligence and creativity.

- A meaningful life aims not so much at day-to-day contentment as fulfilment. We may be leading a meaningful life and yet often be in a bad mood – just as we may be having frequent superficial fun while living, for the most part, meaninglessly.

- A meaningful life is bound up with the long term. Projects, relationships, interests and commitments will build up cumulatively. Meaningful activities leave something behind, even when the emotions that once propelled us into them have passed.

- Meaningful activities aren't necessarily those we do most often. They are those we value most highly and will, from the perspective of our deaths, miss most deeply.

- The question of what makes life meaningful has to be answered personally, even if our conclusions are marked by no particular idiosyncrasy. Others cannot be relied upon to determine what will be meaningful to us. What we call 'crises of meaning' are generally moments when someone else's – perhaps very well-intentioned – interpretation of what might be meaningful to us runs up against a growing realisation of our divergent tastes and interests.

- We have to work out, by a process of experience and introspection, what counts as meaningful in our eyes. Pleasure may manifest itself immediately, but our taste in meaning may be more elusive. We can be relatively far into our lives before we securely identify what imbues them with meaning.

This book considers a range of options to discover where meaning might lie for us. It is anchored around a discussion of eight centrally meaningful activities: love, family, work, friendship, culture, politics, nature and philosophy. Most are well known; the point here is not to identify entirely new sources of meaning so much as to try to evoke and explain some familiar choices.

The options should provide orientation, enabling us to find our own preferences or, when we dissent, to design alternatives.

Along the way, we hope to underscore that our lives are more meaningful – and certainly more capable of meaning – than we might initially suppose. Increasing the amount of meaning in our lives doesn't have to involve any radical outward moves. Our lives almost certainly already have some hugely meaningful aspects to them, but we may not be correctly valuing, understanding or appreciating these. It is time to turn the pursuit of a meaningful life from a comically complex impossibility to something we can all comprehend, aim for and succeed at.

1
Sources of Meaning

i. Love

Care

One way to get a sense of why love should so often be considered close to the meaning of life is to look at the challenges of loneliness. Frequently, we leave the topic of loneliness unmentioned: those without anyone to hold feel shame; those with someone might feel (a background degree of) guilt. But the pains of loneliness are an unembarrassing and universal possibility. We shouldn't feel lonely about being lonely. Unwittingly, loneliness gives us the most eloquent insights into why love matters so much. There are few greater experts on the importance of love than those who are bereft of anyone to love. It is hard to know quite what all the fuss around love might be about until and unless one has, somewhere along the way, spent some bitter, unwanted passages in one's own company.

When we are alone, people may try to show us kindness; there may be invitations and touching gestures, but it will be hard to escape the lingering sense of the conditionality of the interest and care on offer. We are liable to sense the limits of the availability of even the best-disposed companions and sense the restrictions of the demands we can make upon them. It is often too late, or too early, to call. In bleak moments, we may suspect we could disappear off the earth and no one would notice or care. In ordinary company, we cannot simply share whatever is passing through our minds: too much of our inner monologue is overly petty or intense, random or anxiety-laden to be of interest. Our acquaintances have an understandable expectation, which it would be unwise to disabuse them of, that their friends should be normal.

We must operate with a degree of politeness, too. No one finds rage or obsession, peculiarity or bitterness especially charming. We can't act up or rant. A radical editing of our true selves is the price we must pay for conviviality.

We have to accept too that much of who we are won't readily be understood. Some of our deepest concerns will be met with blank incomprehension, boredom or fear. Most people won't care. Our deeper thoughts will be of scant interest. We will have to subsist as pleasant but radically abbreviated paragraphs in the minds of almost everyone.

Love promises to correct all these quietly soul-destroying aspects of single life. In the company of a lover, there need be almost no limits to the depths of concern, care and licence we are granted. We will be accepted more or less as we are; we won't be under pressure to keep proving our status. It will be possible to reveal our vulnerabilities and compulsions and survive. It will be OK to have tantrums, to sing badly or to cry. We will be tolerated if we are less than charming or simply vile for a time. We will be able to wake up our lover at odd hours to share sorrows or excitements. Our smallest scratches will be of interest. We will be able to raise topics of awe-inspiring minuteness (it won't have been like this since early childhood, the last time kindly others expended serious energy discussing whether the top button on our cardigan should be done up or left open).

In the presence of the lover, evaluation will no longer be so swift and cynical. They will lavish time on us. As we tentatively allude to something, they will become eager and excited. They will say 'go on' when we stumble and hesitate. They won't just say 'poor you' and turn away. They will search out relevant details; they will piece together an accurate picture that does justice to our inner lives. The fragile parts of ourselves will be in safe hands. We will feel immense gratitude to this person who does something that we might have come to suspect would be impossible: to know us really well and still like us. We will have escaped from that otherwise dominant and devastating sense that the only way to get people to like us is to conceal most of who we are.

We will start to feel as if we exist. Our identity will be safe; we won't be the only guardians of our story. When the world's disinterest chills and erodes us, we will be able to return to the lover to be put back together again, reflected back to ourselves in terms that reassure and console us. Surrounded on all sides by lesser or greater varieties of coldness, we will at last know that, in the arms of one extraordinary, patient and kindly being worthy of infinite gratitude, we truly matter.

Admiration

In Plato's dialogue *The Symposium* (c. 385–370 BCE), the playwright Aristophanes suggests that the origins of love lie in a desire to complete ourselves by finding a long-lost 'other half'. At the beginning of time, he ventures in playful conjecture, all human beings were hermaphrodites with double backs and flanks, four hands and four legs, and two faces turned in opposite directions on the same head. These hermaphrodites were so powerful and their pride so overweening that Zeus was forced to cut them in two, into a male and a female half – and from that day, each one of us has nostalgically yearned to rejoin the part from which he or she was once severed.

We don't need to buy into the literal story to recognise a symbolic truth: we fall in love with people who promise that they will, in some way, help to make us whole. At the centre of our ecstatic feelings in the early days of love there is gratitude at having found someone who seems to complement our qualities and dispositions. Unlike us, they have (perhaps) a remarkable patience with administrative detail or an invigorating habit of rebelling against officialdom. They may have an ability to keep things in proportion and to avoid hysteria. Or it might be that they have a particularly melancholy and sensitive nature and are in touch with deeper currents of thought and feeling.

We do not all fall in love with the same people because we are not all missing the same things. The aspects that we find desirable in our partners speak of what we admire but do not have secure possession of in ourselves. We may be powerfully drawn to the competent person because we know how our own lives are held up by tendencies to panic around bureaucratic complications. Our love may zero in on the comedic sides of a partner because we're only too aware of our tendencies to sterile despair and cynicism. Or we may be drawn to an atmosphere of thoughtful concentration in a partner as a relief from our own skittish minds.

We love in part in the hope of being helped and redeemed by our lovers. There is an underlying desire for education and growth. We hope to change a little in their presence, becoming, through their help, better versions of ourselves. Just below the surface, love contains a hope for reparation and education. We usually think of education as something harsh imposed upon us against our will, but love promises to educate us in a more gentle and seductive way.

Aware of our lover's qualities, we may allow ourselves some moments of pure rapture and undiluted enthusiasm. The excitement of love stands in contrast with our normal disappointments and scepticism about others; spotting what is wrong with a person is a familiar, quickly completed and painfully unrewarding game. Love gives us the energy to construct and hold onto the very best story about someone. We are returned to a primal gratitude. We are thrilled by apparently minor details: that they have called us; that they are wearing a particular pullover; that they lean their head on their hand in a certain way; that they have a tiny scar over their left index finger or a habit of slightly mispronouncing a word … It isn't usual to take this kind of care over a fellow creature, to notice so many tiny, touching, accomplished and poignant things in another. This is what parents, artists or a god might do. We can't necessarily continue in this vein forever, and the rapture may not be entirely sane, but it is a hugely redemptive pastime – and a kind of art all of its own – to give ourselves over to properly appreciating the real complexity, beauty and virtue of another human being.

Desire

One of the more surprising, and at one level perplexing, aspects of love is that we don't merely wish to admire our partners; we are also powerfully drawn to want to possess them physically. But we can only start to understand the role of sexuality in love if we can accept that it is not just a physical experience that we want.

Sex delivers a major psychological thrill. A lot of our delight has its origin in the idea of being allowed to do a very private thing to and with another person. Another person's body is usually a highly protected and private zone. It would be deeply offensive to go up to a stranger and finger their cheeks or touch them between their legs. The mutual permission involved in sex is dramatic and at the core of our desire. We're implicitly saying to another person through our unclothing that they have been placed in a tiny, intensely policed, category of people; that we have granted them an extraordinary privilege.

Therefore, it is not so much what our bodies do in sex that generates our excitement; it is what happens in our brains. Acceptance is at the centre of the kinds of experiences we collectively refer to as 'getting turned on'. It feels physical: the blood pumps faster, the metabolism shifts gear, the skin gets hot. But behind all this lies a very different kind of pleasure rooted in the mind: a sense of an end to our isolation.

ii. Family

Emotional nepotism

One of the things that makes families so important and so meaningful is that they are centres of unashamed nepotism. We are used to thinking negatively of nepotism. We are taught that a good society is one in which people rise and fall according to their own merits or flaws, and do not gain unfair favour from their families. But, in a crucial emotional sense at least, most of us don't actually believe this. We are all, more or less, emotional nepotists.

Historically, the idea of nepotism in Europe was particularly associated with the Catholic Church during the Renaissance. The word 'nepotism' was born when a series of popes took to appointing their nephews (*nipote* in Italian), along with other family members, to top jobs irrespective of their talents and simply on the basis of their connections.

In 1534, the already elderly Alessandro Farnese was elected pope and took the name Paul III. One of the first things he did was to elevate his young grandson (also called Alessandro) to the influential and lucrative position of cardinal. He made another grandson the duke of one of the small Italian states that was, at that time, directly under the control of the pope. It was all appallingly unfair. In this regard, nepotism presents a deep affront to modern enlightened ideals of open competition, especially around work and careers.

Titian, *Pope Paul III and His Grandsons*, 1545–1546

Nevertheless, we have to admit that the idea of bias towards relatives possesses – in the emotional as opposed to the professional sense – a reassuring and attractive side as well. What's more, we have all already been the beneficiaries of the starkest, grossest nepotism. We wouldn't have got here without it. That's because when we were born, despite the millions of other children in the world, irrespective of our merits (we didn't really have any), our parents and wider family made the decision to take care of us and to devote huge amounts of time, love and money to our well-being. This was not because we had done anything to deserve it – at that time, we were barely capable of holding a spoon, let alone saying hello – but simply because we were related to them.

Nepotism is what ensures that a series of tantrums will be forgiven; that unpleasant traits of character will be overlooked; that we'll be supported as we rant and rage in the small hours; that parents will forgive children who have not been especially good – and that children with somewhat disappointing parents will still, despite everything, show up for the holidays.

Because of the existence of family, we've all experienced belonging, not based on our beliefs, accomplishments or efforts (all of which may change or fail), but on something purer and more irrevocable: the fact of our birth. In a world in which our employment generally hangs by a thread, in which we are judged swiftly and definitively by almost everyone, in our families at least, we know that we can't be sacked, even if we don't make very special conversation at dinner and have failed dismally in our careers. Given how fragile our standing generally is in the eyes of others, this is a source of huge ongoing emotional relief.

Within families, there is often a welcome disregard not just for demerit but for merit as well. Within the family, it may not really matter how badly, or how well, you are doing in the world of money and work. The daughter who becomes a high court judge will probably not be loved any more than the son who has a stall in the market selling origami dragons; the steely negotiator and demanding boss in charge of the livelihoods of thousands may be teased endlessly by their relatives for their poor taste in jumpers or tendency to belch at inopportune moments.

Although nepotism is genuinely misplaced at work, some version of nepotism is extremely important in our emotional lives. However competent and impressive we might be in some areas, there will inevitably be many points at which we are distinctly feeble, and where we urgently need at least a few people to be patient with our failings and follies; to give us a second chance (and a third and a fourth) and to stay on our side even though we don't really deserve it. Good families aren't blind to our faults; they just don't use these faults too harshly against us.

Knowledge

Our family members are probably the only people in the world who ever deeply understand key parts of us. Perhaps we don't always get on better with them than with other people. They might not know the details of our current friendships or the precise state of our finances. But they have a knowledge of the underlying atmosphere of our lives that others will almost certainly lack.

When we make new acquaintances in adult life, we are necessarily meeting relatively late on in our respective developments. We might learn the broad outline of their childhood, but we won't know what the holiday caravan or the beach house were really like; we won't understand the details of the jokes, the smells, the textures of the carpets or the favourite foods, or the finer-grained aspects of the emotions in circulation.

With family members, the knowledge tends to be the other way round. They might not know too much about our present and they weren't necessarily ideally wise or intelligent witnesses, but they were there – which gives them a definitive edge in grasping a great share of who we might be. Relationships in adult life are often complicated by a lack of intimate knowledge of the past. If we had been the brother or sister of the loud, domineering figure we meet for the first time over dinner, we would have understood that they were still, at root, trying to be heard by their inattentive mother. As a result, we would know the perfect response ('I'm listening now') that would instantly have calmed them down. If we had shared a bath with the tough, exacting chief financial officer at work when we were 3, we would know that his highly rigorous, inquisitorial approach (which is so off-putting) was an attempt to stave off the chaos that surrounded him at home after his parents' messy divorce. The full facts would make us much more ready to be patient and generous.

Safe strangeness

One of the reliable horrors, but also profound advantages, of families is that they force us to spend time around people we would otherwise never know about, thought we wanted to meet, or imagined we could get along with.

Our friendships and professional networks are hugely but harmfully efficient at keeping us closely tied to a particular age, income and ideological bracket. We subtly yet firmly expel all those who do not flatter our worldview. Family life does the opposite. It is because of the unique structure of a family that an 82-year-old woman and a 4-year-old boy can become friends or that a 56-year-old dentist and an 11-year-old schoolgirl can have an in-depth conversation about tyre pressure or splash each other at the beach.

The family creates an environment in which there is enough safety to allow for encounters with radical strangeness. A brother-in-law will bring us into contact with life in the Russian diamond market; the university researcher who has just published a paper on the carbon cycle in the Takayama forests of Japan gets to sit down for lunch with an accountant specialising in insolvency cases. And in family settings, points of connection end up being found despite all the obvious differences. We do the dishes with someone whose political views are pretty much the opposite of our own but discover we agree about how to rinse glasses properly. We rescue the picnic from an unexpected downpour with someone who earns eighty-three times more than us serving as our loyal assistant. Prompted by our nieces and nephews, we get into an adult vs. child water gun fight, supported by a cousin whom our friends would dismiss as a long-haired loser but who we realise is great at spotting an opportunity for an ambush.

Families, at their best, hold out against generational segregation: we get to hear the political views of a great-aunt and encounter convictions that were widespread in 1973. We receive an update on the dramas of the junior hockey league; a younger cousin is agonising over school exams and tentatively exploring what they might like to do after turning 21; an uncle has recently retired and is trying to come to terms with a life without work; at the funeral of a grandparent there is an 18-month-old niece crawling around, and we are temporarily connected with the world of changing nappies and messy spoon feeding.

So often, otherness – other stages of life, other attitudes, other outlooks – are presented to us in tricky guises that make it hard for us to engage with them confidently. It is not surprising, or intrinsically shameful, that we are often awkward around people who seem to be quite unlike us, but our picture of them (and hence of ourselves) is thereby drastically impoverished and inaccurate. When family life goes well, on the other hand, we are exposed – at first hand, and in a warm way – to ranges of human experience that might otherwise only be presented to us in caricatured and frightening styles in the course of our independent lives.

Parenthood

Most of our lives are spent in situations of numbing sterility. There is usually no option but to conform and obey impersonal rules. In our work, we don't generally create anything of particular wonder or interest. We don't know how to paint or to play Chopin's Scherzo No. 2 in B flat minor. We can't personally manufacture an iPhone; we don't know how to extract oil from the ground.

And yet, without being conscious of the specifics, we are at points capable of doing something properly miraculous: we can make another person. We can conjure up the limbs and organs of a fellow creature. We can create a liver; we can design someone else's brain; we can – by ingesting a mixed diet perhaps including bananas, cheese sandwiches and ginger biscuits – make fingers; we can connect neurons that will transmit thoughts about the history of the Ancient Persians or the workings of the dishwasher. We can choreograph the birth of an organic machine that might still be going close to 100 years from now. We can be the master coordinator and chief designer of a product more advanced than any technology and more complex and interesting than the greatest work of art.

Having a child definitively refutes any worry about our lack of creativity and dismantles (at least for a while) the envy we might otherwise feel about the inventiveness of others. They may have written a stirring song, started and sold a bioengineering company or plotted an engaging novel. But we will have created the oddest yet most inspiring work of art and science around: one that is alive; one that will develop its own centres of happiness and secrecy; one that will one day do its homework, get a job, hate us, forgive us, end up being, despite itself, a bit like us and, eventually, make humans of its own who can spawn themselves into perpetuity.

However much they may resent one another, grow apart or be worn down by the humdrum nature of family life, parents and children are never entirely able to get past the supernatural sequence of events that connects creators and created. Because two people met fifteen years ago in a friend's kitchen, liked the look of one another, swapped phone numbers and went out for dinner, there is now – across the table – a being with a particular sort of nose, a distinctive emotional temperament and a way of smiling that (as everyone remarks) strikingly echoes that of a dead maternal grandfather.

Parenting demands that one address the greatest, founding philosophical question: what is a good life? As we go about answering it in our words and actions over long years, we will know that we have been spared the one great fear that otherwise haunts us and usually manifests itself around work: that of not being able to make a difference. There will be no danger of lacking impact, only of unwittingly exerting the wrong kind. We will be the biographers, coaches, teachers, chefs, photographers, masters and slaves of our new charges.

Our parental work will lend us the opportunity to show our worst, but also our best, selves in action. It is the particular words we find, the touch of our hands, the encouraging look only we will be able to give, the swerve towards lenience or the brave defence of principles that will make a decisive difference to the sorrows and joys of another human being. Who we are every day, the specific individuals we will have matured into, will have an unparalleled power to exert a beneficial influence on somebody else's life. In our roles as parents, we will be terrified, exhausted, resentful, enchanted, but forever spared the slightest doubt as to our significance or our role on the earth.

iii. Work

Authenticity

The goal of professional life is to do work that is deeply in line with our real selves, that isn't merely about earning our way; that – although it may sometimes be hard and filled with frustrations – answers to the distinctive movements and characters of our own souls. Work that, as we put it, feels properly authentic.

There can be no generalisations about what authentic work will actually require us to do. A job may, for instance, ask us to stick with a set of almost intractable mathematical problems for a long time. This might sound awful to some people, but we may powerfully enjoy the long, slow sense of nibbling away at a major task, trying out many options before landing on an especially good solution. But perhaps authentic work will involve making many urgent and decisive financial interventions in a fast-moving, somewhat chaotic, environment. While this might induce panic in some, for others, calmer circumstances would be hellish. Or it could be that, to feel authentic, we need our work to involve a subordinate, supportive role where we can be admiring of, and loyal to, someone else who is in command – a pleasure stemming back, possibly, to the satisfaction we had as a child around an older, quite bossy, but very impressive sibling.

What makes work authentic is not a particular kind of task; it has nothing to do with making pots or being a carpenter (jobs often superficially associated with the idea of authenticity). What makes work authentic is the deeply individual fit between the nature of our role and our own aptitudes and sources of pleasure.

One of the benefits of having identified authentic work is that we will substantially be freed from envy. There will always be someone doing a job that pays better, that has higher public status or more glamorous fringe benefits. But, we stand to realise, there is no point yearning for such a role, because it would not fit what we know of the distinctive timbre of our own character.

The other benefit to finding work that feels authentic is that it changes our relationship to the modern ideal of achieving work–life balance. There is a degree of pessimism about work within this fashionable concept, for it implies a need to shield life, the precious bit, from the demands of work, the onerous force. But work connected in quite profound ways to who we really are is not the enemy of life: it is the place where we naturally find ourselves wanting to go in order to derive some of our deepest satisfactions.

Meaningful work

We are taught by economics to think of ourselves as, for the most part, selfish creatures. It can seem as if what we primarily want from work is money. What is far more striking is the extent to which we require work to be – as we put it – 'meaningful'. A job can pay well and offer immense prestige, but, unless it is meaningful, it may eventually stifle us and crush our spirits.

What do we mean by 'meaningful' work? It is work that helps others; that has a role to play in making strangers happy. For all that we think of ourselves in darkly egoistic terms, we long for our labours either to reduce the suffering or to increase the pleasure of an audience. We crave a sense that we have left a little corner of the world in slightly better shape as a result of our intelligence and strength. Some jobs fit this requirement with ease; the nurse and the cardiac surgeon are in no doubt as to the meaningful impact of their tasks. But there are less dramatic yet equally soul-warming forms of meaning to be found in a range of less obvious jobs: in sanding someone's floor; in making efficient toothpaste dispensers; in clearing up the accounts; in delivering letters; in teaching someone backhand.

For most of our lives, we are helpless to change circumstances for the better. We are at the mercy of vast impersonal forces over which we have no say. We cannot change the outcome of an election; we cannot prevent a friend making an unfortunate marriage; we cannot resolve the tensions of global politics. But at its best, work pushes against this. In a limited arena, we have agency. We can ensure that someone receives a package on time, understands calculus, eats a well-grilled chicken or sleeps in crisply ironed bedlinen. We can trace a connection between the things we have to do in the coming hours and an eventual modest but real contribution to the improvement of humankind.

What separates a good day from a bad one is not necessarily that we have been without stress or have returned home early. It is that we have derived a tangible impression of having made a difference to the lives of others. It turns out that it is simply not enough to make only ourselves happy.

Teamwork

We are all severely limited creatures. We can only ever become good at a few things, and we can only apply ourselves properly for a certain number of hours each day; we can keep just a select number of issues in view at any point. And although a working life can feel quite long, we only have three or four decades of high-quality effort in us – a blink of an eye in the larger sweep of history.

Ideally, however, the structure within which we do our work moves the balance in an opposite direction: it radically expands upon individual strength and capacity. When we work alongside others (either as the director of combined labour or as a member of a team), our collective powers are extended way beyond anything that one fragile being could ever achieve.

The team is far stronger, wiser, more intelligent and more capable than the people involved within it can ever be, considered one by one. We massively exceed our own strength. In the ideal team, we grasp exactly what we contribute but also how much the project benefits from what others bring to it. However annoying our colleagues may be, our irritation with them is soothed by an awareness that it is precisely their differences that make them adept at particular moves we would be incapable of, and that justifies the unusual efforts we have to make to get along with them. We accept that it is no surprise when we don't like certain types at the office, yet it is via work that we can learn to appreciate their merits in a way we never would in a purely social setting. Through teamwork, our egoism is submerged within a bigger loyalty: we are held together by a shared goal that everyone knows they could never accomplish in isolation.

Our efforts are not even constrained by the limitations of a single working lifespan. In an important sense we cheat death, because our contribution lives on in the efforts and ambitions of our successor members. The best teams reverse the baneful fundamentals of the human condition: through collaboration, they replace the competitive war of all against all; they substitute collective strength for individual weakness; they turn the brevity of our lives into endeavours that outlast us.

Professionalism

One of the most welcome aspects of work is that we do not, in its vicinity, need to be fully ourselves. Most work demands that those who participate in it behave 'professionally', which means that we are not asked to bring the entirety of our characters to the fore. Even though we may be tempted by all kinds of emotions internally, we know we must handle ourselves with calm and reserve – which is not the limitation it may sound like. Sometimes it can be the greatest freedom to have to repress some of what we are.

A certain collective lack of honesty at work can be an intense relief after too long in a domestic atmosphere where everyone feels it is their duty to be the frank and uncensored correspondent of every passing whim. We have the chance to edit ourselves. Our work need not bear the imprint of too much of our human reality.

According to his closest companions, the artist Paul Cézanne was often prickly, irritable and rude. Under the sway of depressed moods, he could grow tyrannical and mean. But none of this was obvious from his work. If we were to judge him from his labours alone, we would see him as deeply patient, confident and mature, with a powerful sense of harmony and balance and a constant empathy for other humans and for nature itself. In a sense, Cézanne's work was better than he was. This is perhaps a definition of what all work can be when it goes well: a more elevated version of the person who created it.

Paul Cézanne, *Montagne Sainte-Victoire with a Large Pine*, c. 1887

The fact that Cézanne could be a rude and difficult person does not detract from his beautiful, harmonious paintings: work gives us all the opportunity to sublimate the trickier parts of our personalities.

This does not just hold true of artistic work. The legal documents sent around the office may bear none of the panic, emotional turmoil and questionable habits of the person who put them together. The shoe shop, with its hushed atmosphere and elegant logo, shows none of the unreasonableness and peculiarity of those who serve in and designed it. The dentist, in her white jacket, is no longer the awkward person she felt herself becoming over the weekend. Work gives us a chance, rare within the overall economy of our lives, to give precedence to our better natures.

Order

The wider world will always be a mess. But around work, we can sometimes have a radically different kind of experience: we get on top of a problem and finally resolve it. We bring order to chaos in a way that we rarely can in any other area of life.

The Zen Buddhist monks of medieval Japan had an intuitive understanding of this kind of benefit to work. They recommended that, in order to achieve peace of mind, members of a monastery regularly rake the gravel of their intricately plotted and bounded temple gardens around Kyoto. Within the confines of a large courtyard space, the monks could bring total coherence and beauty to fruition. It wasn't completely easy. The monks loved to make ambitious patterns of swirls and circles. The lines were often on a very small scale; they might inadvertently tread on a bit they'd already done. They might struggle to keep the rake at just the right angle. It was sometimes maddening, especially when it was autumn and there were leaves everywhere. But it could all be put right eventually. With time, a bit of careful correction and a well-trained hand, they could get everything just as it should be. The problems were real, but they were bounded, and they could be solved.

We are not wrong to love perfection, but it brings us a lot of pain. At its best, our work offers us a patch of gravel that we can rake, a limited space we can make ideally tidy and via which we can fulfil our powerful

Hojo-Teien (Garden of the Abbot's Hall), Tofuku-ji temple, Kyoto, Japan

The order and harmony of a Zen Buddhist garden. Work can offer the sort of structure and discipline that can give us some refuge from the chaos of the wider world.

inner need for order and control – so often thwarted in a wider world beset by defiant unruliness.

Our lives have to be lived in appalling ignorance: we know nothing of when and how we will die; the thoughts of others remain largely hidden from us; we often can't make sense of our own moods; we are driven by excitements and fears we can barely make sense of. But in work, we can build up a very accurate and extensive field of understanding. We can amaze with the precision of our explanations. A wine maker might reveal that the slight taste of caramel comes from the fact that the grapes were left unusually long in the back of the truck just after they were harvested; a picture restorer will point out that a painting was relined, probably in France, in the 1850s; a dance instructor will be able to tell from the way you walk that you sleep on your left side. To the specialist, some small (but not insignificant) aspect of life has no mysteries; they understand why the boiler is leaking, or how voice recognition works, or how an apparently profitable corporation can be on the verge of bankruptcy. The understanding we come to possess via work might not sound especially thrilling in itself. But it speaks to a larger, more metaphysical, theme in human existence. In a small but real way, through our work, we are clearing and cultivating a tiny portion of a wild surrounding forest and turning it into a harmonious, comprehensible garden.

Money

Obviously, making money is one of the most basic reasons why people work. But our culture has tended to emphasise the negative aspects of this. We have inherited a set of concepts that make it easy to formulate the case against personal or corporate economic drive: wage-slavery, profit-gouging, exploitation, greed, selling out, commodification, materialism, cowboy capitalism … and this is just to open the list.

Despite this, financial ambition can be intimately and properly connected to the most praiseworthy and honourable undertakings. Profit, ultimately, is based on insight: it requires identifying the genuine needs of others more clearly and sooner than one's competitors, and meeting them more effectively. Profit is a sign that one's insights have been on track and that the products and services one is offering are truly valued by clients and customers. It is a symptom of having understood the world slightly better than others.

The desire to make money can, of course, be linked to greed or self-indulgence. But the connection is neither necessary nor inevitable. Money is simply a resource that extends the powers of its possessor. Wealth is what Aristotle called an 'executive' virtue: like physical strength or good looks, it increases an individual's sway in the world. Via money, our kindness can be amplified, our wisdom made more consequential, and our ambitions trained on the long term.

Creativity

'Creativity' is one of the most prestigious ideas of modern times. As a result, we often want to feel creative while lamenting that our lives don't give us sufficient opportunities to be so. However, this impression may come down to an unfairly inflated and unhelpfully skewed notion of what creativity actually involves. We are far too focused on creativity's dramatic high points within a narrow, clichéd band of activities, like the writing of a prize-winning novel or the making of a film that receives accolades at Cannes or Berlin. By this standard, almost no one can be creative, and creativity must remain an elite and even freakish anomaly entirely disconnected from ordinary life.

In 1942, Pablo Picasso dismantled an old bicycle and attached the handlebars to the seat to bring out the resemblance to the head of a bull. It is hard not to be charmed. It is a move that helpfully gives us a more accurate idea of creativity. The items Picasso used were familiar to everyone. The key initiative was that he rearranged them to make each part more valuable than it had been in its previous role. This act of combination tends to be central to the creative act. And crucial to this combination was confidence. Many people might previously have noted the resemblance of handlebars to horns or of a seat to a bull's face, but few would have taken their own perceptions seriously. As the American poet Ralph Waldo Emerson (1803–1882) put it: 'In

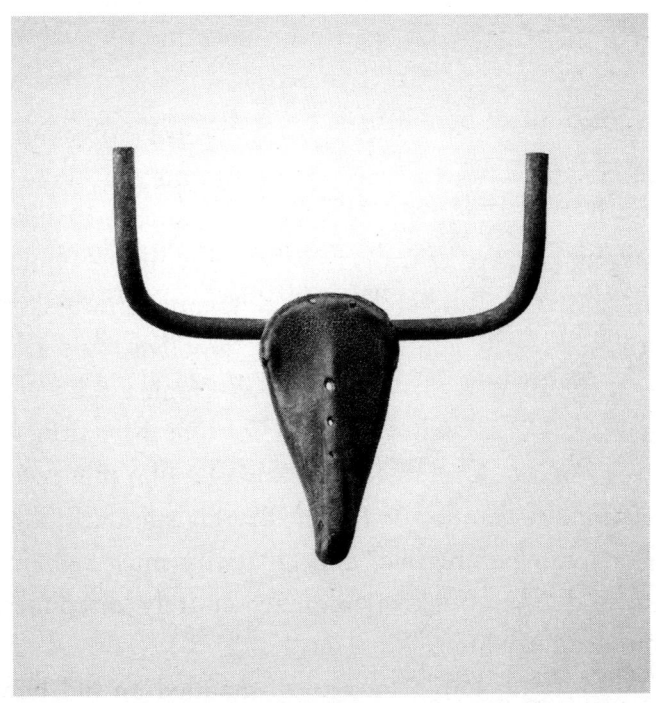

Pablo Picasso, *Tête de Taureau (Bull's Head)*, 1942

Picasso was an exceptionally 'creative' artist. But we can all put into action a basic premise of creativity: the recombination of unlikely elements into something new and unfamiliar.

the minds of geniuses, we find – once more – our own neglected thoughts.' Creative people don't have thoughts fundamentally different from ours; they just don't neglect them as readily.

Very little is entirely new under the sun, but to be creative is to learn to see how apparently unlikely elements might fit together in a fruitful new arrangement. One might borrow a way of organising information from the world of computers and apply it to the management of a gym. One might take an idea associated with the history of Ancient Greece and set it to work within the running of a modern school. One could take a way of speaking that is popular in Japan and collide it with contemporary English diction. Essentially, creativity means spotting an opportunity to improve things through recombination. The German philosopher Georg Wilhelm Friedrich Hegel (1770–1831) put the idea in its grandest terms: we are creative, he wrote, when we 'strip the world of its stubborn foreignness and adapt it to our needs'. Usually, we just put up with matters that are frustrating or disappointing. But when we get creative, we adapt what is to hand – combining, reorganising, starting afresh – so that it better matches our interests and ideals. It is the opposite of feeling stuck and resigned; it is a refusal to accept the status quo. The creative person is someone particularly committed to the idea that there must be a better way of going about things.

A lot of work – both paid and unpaid – is more creative than we usually suppose: when we repaint the bathroom and choose a more pleasing colour that we noticed in a book about houses in India; when we cook a meal and arrange the asparagus on a serving plate in the way they did in a film; when we introduce a set of icons in a report so that the main points come across more clearly; when we put a pot of geraniums we found in the garden centre on the windowsill to make a space more cheerful, or introduce two friends to each other because we've realised how, despite some striking differences, they'll get on well. In every case, we are being creative because we are spotting an opportunity to make an improvement through an act of rearrangement and combination.

Creativity is not a rare and dramatic activity; it is not a sideshow incidental to the core concerns of our lives. Ideally, it is something that we are always involved in. It is a refusal to accept the world as it is in all its facets; it is a commitment to doing better with what we have. As creative people, we don't need to write novels, we just need to be persistently on the lookout for (sometimes very small) ways of improving life.

iv. Friendship

Purpose

Friendship should be an important centre of meaning, and yet it is also a routinely disappointing reality. The key to the problem of friendship is found in an odd-sounding place: we lack a sense of purpose. Our attempts at friendship tend to go adrift because we collectively resist the task of developing a clear picture of what friendship should really be for.

The problem is that we are uncomfortable with the idea of friendship having any declared purpose to begin with, because we associate purpose with the least attractive and most cynical of motives. Yet purpose doesn't have to ruin friendship. In fact, the more we define what a friendship might be for, the more we can focus on what we should be doing with every person in our lives. Indeed, sometimes, we might helpfully conclude that we shouldn't be around someone at all. There is a range of goals we could be pursuing with the people we know. Grasping what the opportunities are is central to building a meaningful social existence.

Networking

Networking has a bad name; it is associated with self-enrichment, egoism and snobbery. But in essence it is a search for help. It springs from a fundamentally modest awareness of how fragile and limited each of us is, and how much we need the support and strength of others.

Networking is only ever as good or bad as the ends to which it is put. There are some very impressive versions of networking in history. The ancient Greek story of the Argonauts tells how the heroic captain Jason travelled around the countryside networking to assemble a band of associates to help him in his search for the legendary Golden Fleece. Jesus of Nazareth networked extensively in order to put together a team of disciples who could help him spread a message about love, redemption and sacrifice.

To network means to filter intelligently, to recognise that one cannot – and indeed should not – try to get to know everyone. It involves aligning one's path through the world with a mission. It implies a wise acknowledgement that we do not have unlimited time.

Ideally, our networks should be wide, diverse and without snobbery, because useful information, valuable skills, perspectives, opportunities and guidance can be located in very unexpected places. In espionage, this key point has been deeply understood: it might be as productive to make contact with the embassy cleaning staff as with the economic attaché; the bartender could be as rich a source of information as the general. We can take this refreshingly open-minded attitude into the world at large. We may learn as much about business from a bankrupt felon as from a successful CEO; the taxi driver may have key things to teach us about life; the person with the woolly hat standing by the bus stop may provide the starting point for a crucial new entrepreneurial idea. With a conscious mission in mind, networking ceases to be a brutal, discriminatory activity. It's just a way of making sure that we are never far from harvesting insights and assistance.

Self-knowledge

One of the oddest and most unhelpful things about being human is that we find it very difficult to know ourselves properly. Theoretically, nothing sounds simpler. We are around ourselves all the time, and we have direct access to our own minds. But, in fact, we often struggle to form an accurate picture of our own character. We feel angry but are not sure why. Something is wrong with our job, but we can't pin it down. We don't realise why we may be quite negative about someone. We don't see when we come across as arrogant or as fawning; at times we find it hard to work out what we really think or what is troubling us. The mind is skittish and squeamish. As a result, many issues lie confused within us.

A true friend notices a lot about us, and has a strong enough hold on our affection and trust to raise issues in a way that we can take them on board. If we let them, they can frame a point not as a devastating criticism but as a sympathetic and generous bit of encouragement to our own better nature. They help us to like ourselves and then to tolerate recognising some less than perfect things about who we are. They take our distress or excitement or anger seriously, but ask gentle and probing questions that help us understand our own initially vague first thoughts and feelings. They listen carefully, and they make it clear that they are on our side. They help us stick with a tricky point and go into more detail; they make connections to something we said earlier; they note our facial expression or tone of voice; they don't jump to fill a pause but wait for us to say more. They act as a judicious, kindly mirror that helps us to know and befriend our own deeper selves.

Fun

Despite talk of hedonism and immediate gratification, life gives us constant lessons in the need to be serious. We have to keep our heads down, avoid looking like a fool and pass as a mature adult. The pressure can become onerous, and in the end even dangerous. That is why we constantly need access to people we can trust enough to be silly with. Most of the time they might be training to be a neurosurgeon or advising medium-sized companies about their tax liabilities but when we are together, we can be therapeutically daft with them. We can put on accents, share lewd fantasies, or doodle on the newspaper, adding a huge nose and a missing front tooth to the president, or giving a model over-large ears and a handlebar moustache.

The fun friend solves the problem of shame around important but unprestigious sides of ourselves. They don't ignore or dismiss our more serious and solemn aspects; they show us that, in their eyes, being silly is not a disgrace: it is a serious need like any other.

Old friends

There are people we are friends with for one major but often maligned or overlooked reason: because we were friends with them some time back. At one stage – and it might be decades ago now – we had a lot in common: we were both good at maths but bad at French at school; we had adjacent rooms at college and helped each other with assignments and commiserated in the bar about failed dates or maddening parents; we were interns in the same big firm with the same bizarre and intemperate boss.

But life has taken us on radically different tracks. Now they've got three young children; they moved to the Orkneys where they are managing a fish farm; they've gone into politics and have become a junior minister, or they're working as a ski teacher in the Rocky Mountains. The daily realities of our lives may be miles apart; we may know little of their world and they of ours. If we were introduced today, we'd think each other pleasant enough but would never get close.

Yet it can be hugely helpful and redemptive to catch up with these people with a one-on-one dinner, a walk in the woods or the occasional email. These friends function as conduits to earlier versions of ourselves that are inaccessible day to day but contain important insights.

In the company of an old friend, we can take stock of the journey we have travelled. We get to see how we have evolved, what was once painful, what mattered or what we had wholly forgotten we deeply enjoyed. The old friend is a guardian of memories on which we might otherwise have a damagingly tenuous hold.

We need old friends because of a crucial complexity in human nature. We pass through stages of development and, as we do so, discard previous concerns and develop a lack of empathy around past perspectives. At 14, we knew a lot about resenting our parents. Twenty years later, the whole idea sounds absurd and ungrateful. Yet the old friend reconnects us with a particular atmosphere and, like a novelist, makes us at home with a character – ourselves – who might otherwise seem impossibly alien to us.

At 22, we found single life extremely painful. We hung out a lot with a particular friend and shared a litany of wistful, alienated thoughts. At 45, with a young family around us, we might occasionally find ourselves curious about the joys of single life and of casual hook-ups. The old friend has crucial news to impart. We experience life from a succession of very different vantage points over the decades, but – understandably – tend to be preoccupied only with the present vista, forgetting the particular, incomplete but still crucial wisdom contained in earlier phases. Every age possesses a superior kind of knowledge in some area, which it usually forgets to hand on to succeeding selves.

Remembering what it was like not to be who we are now is vital to our growth and integrity. The best professors remain friends with their past. They remember what it was like not to know about their special topic, and so don't talk over the heads of their students. The best bosses are in touch with their own experience of starting out as a lowly employee. The best politicians clearly recall periods in their lives when they held very different views to the ones they have now formulated, which allows them to persuade and empathise with hostile constituencies. Good parents keep in touch with the feelings of injustice and sensitivity they had in early childhood. Kindly wealthy people remember what it was like not to dare to walk into a costly food shop. We are always better long-term lovers if we have an avenue of loyalty back to who we were when we first met our beloveds and were at an apogee of gratitude and modesty.

Old friends are key activators of fascinating and valuable parts of the self that we need, but are always at risk of forgetting, in the blinkered present.

A range of friends

Different friends bring to the fore different sides of who we are: they influence us, encourage us and make us feel more at ease in varied ways. With one friend, we become more intellectual than usual; with another more adventurous, or more serious about politics, or more tender towards family. With a wide range of friends within reach, we are able to assemble and connect with the full, properly rounded, version of ourselves.

Every friend has things to teach us; they may not deliver formal lessons, but their point of view and their values are subtly imparted to us. By liking them, their part of the world comes to seem less alien, which is why it is especially interesting and helpful to have friends who give us access to attitudes and social groups that we might otherwise fear or dismiss.

If we are conservatively minded, it is hugely helpful to have a friend who is deeply radical. We might not agree with their ideas, but, because we like them, we don't hold their views in contempt. Or, if we are personally without religious faith, it can be a great benefit to be close to someone who believes. We may not think they are right, but we can, in their company, see how lovely, witty and intelligent someone on the other side can be.

If we can't be friends with someone of opposing views, we will probably never become a powerful advocate of our own convictions, because we will never properly grasp what draws someone to the views we disagree with

– and we will never understand what it would take to change their minds.

Friends give us access to news of vulnerabilities we could never otherwise guess at – and thereby help us to feel less ashamed of, and lonely with, ourselves. We might glimpse the profound worries and sense of alarm of the CEO who is terrified of losing their job if they don't meet their targets; we can hear the van driver with fifteen tattoos talking movingly about their parents and their child; a well-off friend can divulge their inner distress around being thought problem-free; a very beautiful friend can divulge their fear of being patronised and unappreciated. We can gain access to a true vision of normality: the weak are stronger than we suppose; the strong are weaker than we imagine. And our own inevitable failings and idiocies look less alarming against a broader backdrop of sympathetic others.

v. Culture

Home

One of the most meaningful activities we ever engage in is the creation of a home. Over a number of years, typically with a lot of thought and considerable dedication, we assemble furniture, crockery, pictures, rugs, cushions, vases, sideboards, taps, door handles and so on into a distinctive constellation that we anoint with the word 'home'. As we create our rooms, we engage passionately with culture in a way we seldom do in the supposedly higher realms of museums or galleries. We reflect profoundly on the atmosphere of a picture; we ponder the relationship between colours on a wall; we notice how consequential the angle of the back of a sofa can be and ask carefully what books truly deserve our ongoing attention.

Our homes will not necessarily be the most attractive or sumptuous environments we could spend time in. There are always hotels or public spaces that would be a good deal more impressive. But after we have been travelling a long while, after too many nights in hotel rooms or on the beds of friends, we typically feel a powerful ache to return to our own furnishings – an ache that has little to do with material comfort per se. We need to get home to remember who we are.

Our homes have a memorialising function, and what they help us to remember is, strangely enough, ourselves. We can see this need to anchor identity in matter in the history of religion. From the earliest days, humans have expended enormous care and creativity on building homes for their gods. They haven't felt that their gods could live just anywhere, out in the wild or (as it were) in hotels; they have believed that they needed special places, temple-homes, where their specific characters could be stabilised through art and architecture.

For the Ancient Greeks, Athena was the goddess of wisdom, rationality and harmony, and in 420 BCE, they completed a home for her on the slopes of the Acropolis. It wasn't a large home, but it was an exceptionally apt and beautiful one. The temple felt dignified but approachable. It was rigorously balanced and logical, serene and poised. It was its inhabitant artfully sculpted in limestone.

The Greeks took such care over Athena's temple-home because they understood the human mind. They knew that, without architecture, we struggle to remember what we care about – and more broadly who we are. To be told in words that Athena represented grace and balance was not enough on its own. There needed to be a house to bring the idea forcefully and continuously to consciousness.

Without there being anything grandiose or supernatural in the idea, our homes are also temples; they are temples to us. We are not expecting to be worshipped, but we are trying to make a place that – like a temple – adequately embodies our spiritual values and merits.

Creating a home is frequently such a demanding process because it requires us to find our way to objects

Culture

The temple of Athena on the Acropolis of Athens

The Greeks created Athena's temple-home to represent in architecture what she represented as a deity: grace, balance, wisdom and harmony. We can create our own temple-homes to embody our own values and characteristics.

that can correctly convey our identities. We may have to go to enormous efforts to track down what we deem to be the 'right' objects for particular functions, rejecting hundreds of alternatives that would in a material sense be perfectly serviceable, in the name of those we believe can faithfully communicate the right messages about who we are. We become fussy because objects are, in their own ways, all hugely eloquent. Two chairs that perform much the same physical role can articulate entirely different visions of life.

One chair by the Swiss 20th-century architect Le Corbusier speaks of efficiency, excitement about the future, international spirit, impatience around nostalgia and devotion to reason. The other, by the English 19th-century designer William Morris, speaks of the superiority of the pre-industrial world, the beauty of tradition, the appeal of patience and the pull of the local. We may not play out such precise scripts in our heads when we see the chairs, but, just below the threshold of consciousness, we may be highly responsive to the messages that such objects beam out to the world.

An object feels 'right' when it speaks attractively about qualities that we are drawn to, but don't possess strong enough doses of in our day-to-day lives. The desirable object gives us a more secure hold on values that are present, yet fragile, in ourselves; it endorses and encourages important themes in us. The smallest things in our homes whisper to us; they offer us encouragement,

(Left) Armchair made for Morris & Co. c. 1864–1965 (stained ash with rush seat), probably designed by Ford Madox Brown (1821–1893) after chairs from Sussex

(Right) Le Corbusier, Pierre Jeanneret and Charlotte Perriand, *Fauteuil B 301*, 1928

reminders, consoling thoughts, warnings or correctives, as we make breakfast or do the accounts in the evening.

Because we all want and need to hear such different things, we will all be pulled towards very different kinds of objects. There is a deeply subjective side to the feeling of beauty. However, our conflicts about taste are not arbitrary or random: they are grounded in the fact that the kinds of messages we benefit from being exposed to will vary depending upon what is tentative and under threat in our own lives.

The quest to build a home is connected to a need to stabilise and organise our complex selves. It is not enough to know who we are in our own minds; we need something more tangible, material and sensuous to pin down the diverse and intermittent aspects of our identities. We need to rely on certain kinds of cutlery, bookshelves, laundry cupboards and armchairs to align us with who we are and seek to be. We are not vaunting ourselves; we are trying to gather our identities in one receptacle, preserving ourselves from erosion and dispersal. Home means the place where our soul feels that it has found its proper physical container, where, every day, the objects we live among quietly remind us of our most authentic commitments and loves.

Music

Music is of central importance to most of us, but we are extremely picky not just about what music we listen to, but also when we do so. At a given point, we will really want to listen to a Bach cantata; at another it has to be The Supremes. One evening, a song by Fleetwood Mac keeps calling for us; on a second evening, we are impatient to hear a particular Mozart aria. Why do these different modulations and sequences of sound seem so important to us at specific moments, and not so much at others?

To understand why, we need to focus on a peculiar but crucial fact about ourselves. We are highly emotional beings, but not all of our emotions make their way to the front of our conscious attention when they need to. They are there, but only in a latent, muted, undeveloped way. There is too much noise both externally and internally: we are under pressure at work; there's a lot to be done at home; the news is on, we're catching up with friends.

Yet in the background, we may be storing up the ingredients for a range of profound and potentially very important emotions: the raw matter for grief, sorrow, a sense of tender generosity towards humanity in general, a quiet sense of the beauty of modesty or pity for ourselves – for all the errors we didn't mean to make, all the ways we've wasted our own best potential and didn't properly return love when it was offered ... These feelings and many others are the emotional containers of profound wisdom.

But they may not have the sway they ideally should in our lives because they don't receive sustained attention and an opportunity to develop. They exist as confused, weak signals in us – hardly noticeable, easily disregarded blips of sensation; raw matter that has not been catalysed. And so, the beauty, goodness, consolation and strength they could bring us never quite emerge; we bear within us a legacy of unfelt feelings.

This is why music matters: it offers amplification and encouragement. Specific pieces of music give strength and support to valuable but tentative emotional dispositions. A euphoric song amplifies the faint but ecstatic feeling that we could love everyone and find true delight in being alive. Day to day, these feelings exist, but are buried by the pressure to be limited, cautious and reserved. Now the song pushes them forward and gives them confidence; it provides the space in which they can grow and, given this encouragement, we can accord them a bigger place in our lives.

A sombre, tender piece may coax to the surface our submerged sadness. Under its encouraging tutelage, we can more easily feel sorry for the ways in which we have hurt others; we can pay greater attention to our own inner pain, and hence be more appreciative of small acts of gentleness from friends; we become more alive to universal suffering: that everyone loses the things they love; that everyone is burdened with regrets. With the help of particular chords, a compassionate side of ourselves, which is normally hard to access, becomes more prominent.

A different kind of music might take up our low-key impulses to action and self-transformation: it rouses us; it quickens our pace. We want to stride to its beat and make the best use of our energies while there is still time. Other songs could boost our fragile sense that certain things don't matter all that much: the meeting didn't go very well, but so what? In the end, it's not that important. The kitchen was a bit messy, but it's not a big deal in the cosmic scheme. Our reserves of perspective are activated; we are fortified in our capacity to cope with the petty irritations that would otherwise undermine us.

Like an amplifier with its signal, music doesn't invent emotion; it takes what is there and makes it louder. One might worry that boosting an emotion might at points be risky. After all, not everything we feel is worthy of encouragement. It is possible to use music to magnify feelings of hatred or to inflate violent impulses – and the culture ministries of fascist dictatorships have been fatefully skilled at doing just this. But almost always, we face a very different issue around music: we are not building up our courage to lay waste to civilisation; we just want to strengthen our capacities for calm, forgiveness, love and appreciation.

In our relationship to music, we are seeking the right soundtrack for our lives. A soundtrack in a film helps accord the due emotional resonance to a specific scene. It helps us register the pathos of a situation that might be missed if we relied on words and images alone; it helps us fully recognise the identity of a moment. Exactly the same is true in our lives: we are constantly faced with situations where something significant is going on; at the back of our minds the helpful emotional reaction is there, but it's subdued and drowned out by the ambient noise of existence. Music is the opposite of noise: it is the cure for noise. By finding the right piece of music at the right time, we are adding an accompanying score that highlights the emotions we should be feeling more strongly, and allows our own best reactions to be more prominent and secure. We end up feeling the emotions that are our due. We live according to what we actually need to feel.

Books

Around 130 million books have been published in the history of humanity; a heavy reader will at best get through 6,000 in a lifetime. Most of them won't be much fun or very memorable. Books are like people; we meet many but fall in love very seldom. Perhaps only thirty books will ever truly mark us. They will be different for each of us, but the way in which they affect us will be similar. The core, and perhaps unexpected, thing that books do for us is simplify. It sounds odd, because we think of literature as sophisticated. But there are powerful ways in which books organise and clarify our concerns – and in this sense simplify them.

Centrally, by telling a story, a book is radically simpler than lived experience. The writer omits a huge amount of detail that could have been included. In the plot, we move from one important moment directly to the next, whereas in life there are endless subplots that distract and confuse us. In a story, the key events of a marriage unfold across a few dozen pages. In life, they are spread over many years and interleaved with hundreds of business meetings, holidays, hours spent watching television, chats with one's parents, shopping trips and dentist's appointments. The compressed logic of a plot corrects the chaos of existence: the links between events can be made much more obvious. We finally understand what is going on.

Writers often do a lot of explaining along the way. They frequently shed light on why a character is acting as they do; they reveal people's secret thoughts and motives. The characters are much more clearly defined than the acquaintances we encounter. On the page, we meet purer villains, braver and more resourceful heroes, people whose suffering is more obvious or whose virtues are more striking than would ever be the case normally. They and their actions provide us with simplified targets for our emotional lives. We can love or revile them, pity or condemn them more neatly than the humans around us. We need simplification because our minds become checkmated by the complexity of our lives. The writer, on rare but hugely significant occasions, puts into words feelings that have long eluded us; they know us better than we know ourselves. They seem to be narrating our own stories, but with more clarity than we could ever achieve.

Literature corrects our native inarticulacy. So often we feel lost for words. We are impressed by the sight of a bird wheeling in the dusk sky; we are aware of a particular atmosphere at dawn; we love someone's slightly wild but sympathetic manner. Yet, we struggle to verbalise our feelings; we may end up remarking: 'that's so nice'. Our feelings seem too complex, subtle, vague and elusive for us to be able to spell out. The ideal writer homes in on a few striking things: the angle of the wing; the slow movement of the largest branch of a tree; the angle of the mouth in a smile. Simplification does not betray the nuance of life: it renders life more visible.

The great writers build bridges to people we might otherwise have dismissed as unfeasibly strange or unsympathetic. They cut through to the common core of experience. By selection and emphasis, they reveal the important things we share. They show us where to look.

They also help us to feel. Often we want to be good, we want to care, we want to feel warmly and tenderly, but can't. It seems there is no suitable receptacle in our ordinary lives into which our emotions can vent themselves. Our relationships are too compromised and fraught. It can feel too risky to be very nice to someone who might not reciprocate. So we don't do much feeling; we freeze over. But then, in the pages of a story, we meet someone. Perhaps she is very beautiful, tender, sensitive, young and dying; we weep for her and all the cruelty and injustice of the world. And we come away, not devastated, but refreshed. Our emotional muscles have been exercised and their strength rendered newly available for our lives.

Not all books contain the simplifications we happen to need. We are often not in the right place to make use of the knowledge a book has to offer. The task of linking the right book to the right person at the right time hasn't yet received the attention it deserves. Newspapers and friends recommend books to us because they work for them, without thinking through why they might also work for us. But when we come across the ideal book for us, we are presented with a clearer, more lucid, better organised account of our own concerns and experiences. For a time at least, our minds become less clouded and our hearts more accurately sensitive. Through books' benign simplification, we become a little better at being who we truly are.

Clothes

Once, we were all dressed by someone else. Parents picked out a pair of trousers; the school dictated what colour our shirts should be. But at some point, we were granted the opportunity to discover who we might be in the world of clothes. We had to decide for ourselves about collars and necklines, fit, colours, patterns, textures and what goes with what. We learnt to speak about ourselves in the language of garments. Despite the potential silliness and exaggeration of sections of the fashion industry, assembling a wardrobe is a serious and meaningful exercise.

Based on our looks, background, job, others are liable to come to quick and not very rounded decisions about who we are. Only too often, their judgement doesn't quite get us right. They might assume that, because of where we come from, we must be snobbish or resentful; based on our work, we might get typecast as dour or superficial; the fact that we're sporty might lead people to see us as not terribly cerebral; an attachment to a particular political outlook might be associated with being earnest or cruel.

Clothes provide us with an opportunity to correct some of these assumptions. When we get dressed, we are, in effect, operating as a tour guide, offering to show people around ourselves. We highlight interesting or attractive things about who we are – and, in the process, we clear up misconceptions. We act like artists painting a self-portrait: deliberately guiding the viewer's perception of who we might be.

In 1961, the English painter Peter Blake portrayed himself wearing a denim jacket, jeans and trainers. He was deliberately nuancing the view that most of his contemporaries would have had of him, knowing that he was a successful and rather intellectual painter. He might have been thought of as aloof and refined – detached from, and censorious of, ordinary life. But his clothes speak about very different aspects of his personality: they tell us that he's quite modest; he's interested in pop music; he sees his art as a kind of manual labour. His clothes – like ours – give us a crucial introduction to the self.

This explains the curious phenomenon whereby, if we're staying with good friends, we can spend a lot less time thinking about our clothes, compared with the anxiety about what to wear that can grip us at other points. We might sit around in a dressing gown or just slip on any old jumper. They know who we are already; they are not relying on our clothes for clues.

It is a strange but profound fact that certain items of clothing can excite us. When we put them on or see others wearing them, we're turned on. A particular style of jacket, the right kind of shoes or the perfect shirt might prove so erotic we could almost do without a person wearing them. It is tempting to see this kind of fetishism as deluded, but it alerts us in an exaggerated way to a very normal idea: that certain clothes make us really happy. They capture values that we're drawn to. The erotic component is just an extension of a more general and understandable sympathy. The French novelist Stendhal

Peter Blake, *Self-Portrait with Badges*, 1961

Blake's clothes here are expressing the humbler, more down-to-earth aspects of his personality, when many contemporaries regarded him as aloof, high-brow and intellectual. Our clothing, too, can offer a fuller portrait of our inner selves.

(1783–1842) wrote: 'Beauty is the promise of happiness', and every item of clothing we're drawn to contains an allusion to a different sort of happiness. We might see a desirable kind of confidence in a particular pair of boots; we might meet generosity in a woollen coat or a touching kind of innocence in a hemline; a given watch strap may sum up dignity; the way a specific collar encases the neck could strike us as charmingly commanding and authoritative.

The classic fetishist might be pushing their particular attachments to a maximum and be rather restricted in the choice of items they favour, but they are latching onto a general theme: clothes embody values that enchant and beguile us. By choosing particular sorts of clothes, we are shoring up our more fragile or tentative characteristics. We are communicating to others who we are while strategically reminding ourselves. Our wardrobes contain some of our most carefully written lines of autobiography.

Travel

When approached in the right way, travel can play a critical role in helping us to evolve; it can correct the imbalances and immaturities of our nature, open our eyes, restore perspective, and function as the most meaningful agent of maturation.

Yet in order to work its therapeutic effect, we may need to change how we travel, starting with how we go about choosing our destinations. We are usually badly served by the travel industry, which cuts up the world into material categories unattuned to the needs of our inner selves or, to put it more grandly, our souls. The industry lays before us options like 'outdoor fun', 'family adventure', 'culture weekends' or 'island hideaways', but leaves unexplored what the point of these destinations might be when considered from the point of view of our psyches.

Without anything mystical being meant by this, all of us are involved in what could be termed 'an inner journey': that is, we are trying to develop in particular ways. We might be searching for how to be calmer or to find a way to rethink our goals; we might long for a greater sense of confidence or an escape from debilitating feelings of envy. Ideally, where we go should help us with our attempts at these longed-for pieces of psychological evolution. The outer journey should assist us with the inner one.

This idea comes from an unusual source: the history of religious pilgrimage. Religions have traditionally shown a surprising degree of sympathy for our impulse to travel. They have accepted that we cannot develop our souls just by staying at home. They have insisted – with what can now seem like an alien intensity – on the gravity of going on a trip. They have channelled the raw impulse to take off into a myriad of traditions and rituals, whose examination could prompt us to reflect on our own habits.

In the Middle Ages, Catholicism believed that every ailment of the mind or body could be cured by going off on a long journey to touch a part of the body of a long-dead saint. The church had to hand a dictionary of pilgrimage destinations, which in every case matched problems with solutions. For example, if you were having trouble breast-feeding, France alone offered mothers a choice of forty-six pilgrimages to sanctuaries of Mary's Holy Breast Milk ('Had the Virgin been a cow,' observed the 16th-century Protestant John Calvin unkindly, 'she scarcely could have produced such a quantity').

Believers with a painful molar were advised to travel to Rome to the Basilica of San Lorenzo, where they would touch the arm bones of Saint Apollonia, the patron saint of teeth. If such a trip were awkward, they might go and find pieces of her jaw in the Jesuit church at Antwerp, some of her hair at Saint Augustine's in Brussels, or her toes at disparate sites around Cologne. Unhappily married women were directed to travel to Umbria to touch the shrine of Saint Rita of Cascia, patron saint of marital problems (and lost causes). Soldiers looking to embolden themselves before a battle could commune with the bones of Sainte Foy in a gold-plated reliquary in the abbey-church in Conques in southwestern France. People who worried excessively about lightning could gain relief by travelling to the Jesuit church in Bad Münstereifel in Germany and lay hands on the relics of Saint Donatus, believed to offer help against fires and explosions of all kinds.

Although most of us no longer believe in the divine power of journeys to cure toothache or gallstones, we can still retain the idea that certain parts of the world possess a power to address complaints of our psyches and bring about change in us in a way that wouldn't be possible if we stayed at home. There are places that, by virtue of their remoteness, vastness, climate, chaotic energy, haunting melancholy or sheer difference from our homelands can salve the wounded parts of us. These sites, valuable rather than holy, help us to recover perspective, reorder our ambitions, quell our paranoias and remind us of the interest and obliging unexpectedness of life.

Although we might agree with this at a general level, we still lack a tradition of approaching travel from a properly therapeutic perspective and so of analysing landscapes according to their inner benefits. We lack atlases of destinations with which to treat ourselves. There are as yet no psychotherapeutic travel agencies; no experts in both neurotic disorders and tourism; in the psyche and in the nature trails, museums, hot springs and bird sanctuaries of six continents.

For this to happen, we need to be clearer about both what we're searching for inside and what the outer world could conceivably deliver for us. In part, this requires us to look at the globe in a new way. Every destination we might alight upon contains within it qualities that could conceivably support some move or other on an inner journey. There are places that could help with shyness and others with anxiety. Some places might be good at reducing egoism and others might be good for helping us think more clearly about our careers.

In a meaningful life, we would ideally be more conscious travellers – aware that we were on a search for places that can deliver psychological virtues like 'calm' or 'perspective', 'sensuality' or 'rigour'. A visitor to Monument Valley wouldn't just be there for the sake of undefined 'adventure'; something to enjoy and then gradually forget about. Travelling to the place would be an occasion fundamentally to reorient their personality. It would be the call to arms to become a different person; a secular pilgrimage properly anchored around a stage of character development.

Travel should not be allowed to escape the underlying seriousness of the area of life with which it deals. We should aim for locations in the outer world that can push us towards the places we need to go to within.

vi. Politics

We live in societies in which it is difficult to count as a good and intelligent adult without seeming to take a deep and fairly constant interest in politics. There is a never-ending stream of reliable and penetrating bulletins about the latest events in parliament, law courts, bureaucracies, battlefields and markets. It is not really a viable option to fail to know, or care, about 'what is happening' in the world.

And yet, in the privacy of our hearts, some of us don't care – or not as much as we feel we should. We may follow the constant political fights closely enough. We may even understand the characters; we have some feelings about the key players; we know the tussles between the left and the right, and yet, much of the time, politics may all feel remote and far from anything we would recognise as meaningful. We suppose (perhaps a touch guiltily) that, for whatever reason, the political gene has passed us by.

This may be an unfair conclusion. Almost all of us are intensely political; we just don't recognise ourselves as such because we have been equipped with the wrong definition of politics. We have been taught that 'being political' means having a position on the left–right axis and a daily fascination for those events defined as political by the news industry. But this captures only a small part of what truly constitutes the 'political', when properly understood.

Being political doesn't only or principally mean caring what party wins the next election; to be political is to care about the happiness of strangers. Of course, supporters of a given party or economic doctrine will count as political under this title – they want to win or to push forward tax changes for the good of others, although this motive can get lost in the noise. However, there are plenty of ways in which one may be involved in the task of promoting the happiness of strangers, and therefore immersed in politics as the field should be properly understood.

At a sombre moment in the Peloponnesian War, the ancient Athenian statesman Pericles (d. 429 BCE) made a speech, known as the Funeral Oration, in which he attempted to define what made Athenian society so admirable and so worth fighting and dying for. He covered territory that might sound unfamiliar today. He praised his fellow citizens for their attitudes to beauty, for the way they approached exercise, for the manner in which they entertained each other at home, for their sensitivity to their natural surroundings and for the open, polite manner they had in public places. In Pericles's eyes, all of these were profoundly political topics because they helped define the character of collective life: a political cause might not sound political and yet still be worthy of the name.

With a more Periclean definition of politics in mind, we can see that it could be possible to count as a political person while being principally interested in woodland flowers, psychotherapy, street lamp design, self-knowledge, correct punctuation, politeness, dental hygiene, self-understanding, hiking, humour, architecture, meditation, birdsong, cycle helmets, local history, and a good many other topics besides. We should not let politics be kidnapped by people with an impoverished sense of what the collective good might be.

Part of the reason why being interested in politics has traditionally had high prestige is that it seems a selfless act, a noble prioritising of communal over personal interests. But this too may be an unhelpful starting point, because it privileges a sacrificial impulse that few of us reliably experience. In reality, being political need have nothing to do with self-renunciation. Making strangers happy is deeply enjoyable, and a great deal easier than trying to make oneself or one's immediate loved ones content.

Living in our own minds, we have a constant experience of impotence and failure. Much the same may hold true of our relationships with those close to us. We know how often our initiatives go nowhere, our plans are rebuffed, our intentions are ground down. Politics is a refuge from the problems of trying to make oneself and one's loved ones smile. It is the best possible kind of selfishness.

Acting politically, we can bring our most competent, purposeful selves to bear on a relatively limited set of issues in the lives of strangers, and therefore have a chance of succeeding. We are not trying to solve all the problems of others; we are merely working on one or two targeted areas and so are granted a precious encounter with ourselves as people with the will, imagination and intelligence to get things done. We are taken out of the morass of our own minds. We have the joy of trying to change the world, rather than wrestling with the far thornier task of wondering how to be happy.

vii. Nature

Otherness

We are back from work unusually late. It has been a tricky day: a threatened resignation, an enraged supplier, a lost document, two delayed trains ... But none of the mayhem is of any concern to one friend waiting by the door, uncomplicatedly pleased to see us: Pippi, a 2-year-old Border terrier with an appetite for catching a deflated football in her jaws. She wants to play in the usual way, even if it's past 9 o'clock now, with us in the chair and her sliding around the kitchen, and, unexpectedly, so do we. We are not offended by her lack of overall interest in us. It is at the root of our delight. Here, at last, is someone wholly indifferent to almost everything about us except for our dexterity at ball throwing; someone who doesn't care about the Brussels meeting, who will forgive us for not warning the finance department in time about the tax rebates, and for whom the Singapore conference is beyond imagining.

One of the most consoling aspects of natural phenomena – whether a dog, a sheep, a tree or a valley – is that their meanings have nothing to do with our own perilous and tortured priorities. They are redemptively unconcerned with everything we are and want. They implicitly mock our self-importance and absorption and so return us to a fairer, more modest, sense of our role on the planet.

A sheep knows nothing about our feelings of jealousy; it has no interest in our humiliation and bitterness around a colleague; it has never emailed. On a walk in the hills, it simply ambles towards the path we're on and looks curiously at us, then takes a lazy mouthful of grass, chewing from the side of its mouth as though it were gum. One of its companions approaches and sits next to it, wool to wool, and for a second, they exchange what appears to be a knowing, mildly amused glance.

Beyond the sheep are a couple of oak trees. They are of especially noble bearing. They gather their lower branches tightly under themselves while their upper branches grow in small, orderly steps, producing rich green foliage in an almost perfect circle. It doesn't matter what the election results are, or what happens to the stock market or in the final exams. The same things would have been going on when Napoleon was leading his armies across Europe or when the first nomads made their way towards the Appalachian hills.

Our encounter with nature calms us because none of our troubles, disappointments or hopes has any relevance to it. Everything that happens to us, or that we do, is of no consequence whatever from the point of view of the dog, the sheep, the trees, the clouds or the stars; they are important representatives of a different perspective within which our own concerns are mercifully irrelevant.

Sport

For long stretches of our lives, our bodies steadfastly refuse to obey our commands. As babies, the spoon drops straight out of our hand. Our legs can't hold us up. Our head can't support itself. A little later, as small children, it's pretty hard to do up our shoelaces, and we feel as if we are drowning during our first length down the pool. Then, with age, new failures of coordination begin to dog us: we can't touch our toes; there is a permanent pain in our backs; we can't open a jam jar; we start falling over in the shower.

But in the middle years, we can – in specific contexts – achieve an awe-inspiring degree of mastery over our physical selves. In relation to some closely regulated challenges, we can train our bodies to follow our will entirely. Sport embodies a grand metaphysical struggle of the human spirit against the unruly and entropic forces of the material world. It is the most sophisticated and impressive form of revenge against the humiliations of having a body.

All sports, however outwardly different, have as their goal the masterful subjugation of the body to the will. The Discobolus (Discus Thrower) fashioned by the Greek sculptor Myron in the 5th century BCE shows a man in total command of his body: his thighs, shoulders, turn of the neck, ankles and fingers are all harmonised in the service of throwing the discus as far as possible to the other end of a field.

The Discobolus Lancellotti, Roman copy in marble of a
5th-century BCE Greek original by Myron

This sculpture captures a moment of perfect physical coordination and potential energy. Training the body in an athletic pursuit can give us a glorious sense of physical mastery and momentary perfection.

We see a similar underlying idea of perfect co-ordination and control in all athletic poses: the runner at the starting blocks, the swimmer in mid-stroke or the golfer at the end of a swing. It is a strange and poignant moment to experience ourselves in this masterful way. In an act of scarcely believable precision, on a golf course, a tiny white ball that might have gone pretty much anywhere – into the pond, into the trees, towards a salesman in the clubhouse – can be made to fly 400 yards through the air to come cleanly to rest inside a small, barely visible hole on a highly manicured lawn on the opposite side of a hill.

So often we are clumsy and weak: our own legs won't obey us, our fingers drop glasses, we slip on patches of black ice. But at the high points of our sporting lives, we have the opposite experience: the tennis smash does land exactly in the backhand corner as we'd intended. In mid-stride, we take instantaneous aim, and the long kick does float beautifully, as we'd planned, past the goalkeeper and into the top of the net.

Being a spectator of sport also offers us correctives to some of the entrenched, powerful problems of our lives. For example, it compresses action so as to give us a result within a timeframe in tune with our native impatience and need for resolutions. So often, beyond sport, events move in irritatingly diffuse, chaotic and multiple ways. We lose the thread and therefore the capacity to care. A project may come right in three years' time. If we're lucky, our business may take a decision next April. There are 2,000 people on our team in five time zones. But sport speeds up and edits drama. The results appear precisely on schedule: after ten seconds in the 100 metres; after ninety minutes in a game of football.

Sport also gives us a corrective to the normal pressure to be emotionally guarded, empathetic and intelligently ambivalent. In ordinary life, we're not meant to take sides too strongly. We're always supposed to imagine what bit of the truth may lie with the opposition. But at least briefly, around sport, we can be wholly and wildly partisan. We can innocently long to eradicate the enemy. We don't need to worry about causing offence or about missing a nuance to the argument. We have at last found something pure, good and mercifully simple to believe in.

We can be at odds with almost everyone over issues from the proper direction for the economy to what we should do with the holidays. There is no end to conflict and divergent convictions. But in sport, a devotion to our side brings with it a powerful experience of agreement with large numbers of people we don't know. We're no longer fighting our individual corners: we all agree. We're excited at the same moment; when a questionable decision is made by the judges or umpire, we're outraged by the same injustice. We love some very unlikely strangers.

In our excitement, differences in status are erased. We are all spectators and supporters of the same team. Our job description (always a painfully skewed reflection of who we really are) can be forgotten. The rest of life is suspended; the CEO cheers alongside the stay-at-home father; the timid individual's favourite midfielder makes a glorious, fearless comeback; the corporate chieftain's beloved team is crushed.

The temper of modern life suggests that there is only one person who truly counts: you. Your career, your appearance, your spending power, your house, your car, perhaps your kids and your partner too. Then suddenly, around a big sporting event, you may find you care with extraordinary intensity about the fate of a group of your muscular country folk on a pitch or track far away, jumping remarkably high or passing a ball between one another with dexterity. It takes the pressure off us. It lightens the oppressive responsibility we otherwise feel to ensure that our own lives are stellar. We can find greatness in a mighty cause. We can be proud to belong in a very minor way to an inspiring collective enterprise. Through sport, we have the chance to transcend the clumsier, more mean-spirited, tentative and segregated aspects of our lives.

viii. Philosophy

There are some of us who regularly feel a powerful need to go away and think rather more than is typically allowed or taken to be normal. This business of thinking can seem to us like one of the most meaningful things we ever do. After too long in company, we crave to be alone with our own minds. Raw experience proves too overwhelming, dense, messy, confused or exciting, and, on a regular basis, we long to sort through it, far away from distractions. We stay up late, ruminate in the bath, wake up early, write down our thoughts, go for a walk, and feel perceptibly lightened and refreshed by the process of mastering emotions and the alchemy of converting feelings into ideas. Without anything grandiose being meant by the word, we are driven to philosophise, implicitly siding with Socrates's dictum that the unanalysed life is not worth living, or at least is rather uncomfortable.

We need to remove ourselves and think because, on certain days, we are sad, and yet can't identify the cause of an upset that lingers powerfully somewhere in our minds, just out of reach of consciousness. The more we leave the sadness unattended, the more it starts to colour everything we are involved with. Our experiences become tasteless; a mute fog descends over consciousness. Or else we feel confusedly anxious. Our thoughts refuse to settle. We try to find relief by escaping from ourselves with our phone or a game. Our eyelid starts to twitch; we gnaw at a patch of hard skin on a finger. Our mind knows there are matters we should be focusing on, but they elude understanding and spread their nervous electricity across the range of our thoughts. We may feel irritable; we snap and fly into a sudden rage, knowing it cannot truly be the socks on the floor or the unexpectedly squeaky front door that justify our fury, while hampered by pride or defensive denial from understanding more. Or, in a positive vein, we may feel a mysterious excitement because we hear of a highly original project masterminded by a friend, or read of a new kind of enterprise or see a thought-provoking documentary. Something is calling out to us from within our excitement. We are being sensibly, but inarticulately, summoned in a new direction. The excitement doesn't leave us alone, but nor does it say in plain terms what it wants.

In such contexts, we retreat to think. We have a pen and paper handy on an armchair at home or we are on a train with an expansive view and two hours to talk with ourselves. We return to the contents of our minds and systematically attend to the garbled signals that we patiently submit to the beam of reason. Of our anxious feelings, we ask what steps we need to take, what others have to do, what needs to happen and when. Of our hurt, sad and angry feelings, we dare to dwell on our constant, surprising vulnerability. Perhaps it was a face we briefly saw in the line at the airport that seemed kindly and understanding and evoked some tender, vital things missing from our current relationship. Perhaps it was a quietly ungenerous message we received from a friend, in which we sensed a bitter and wounding rivalry. Or maybe it was a regret, on seeing a sunny landscape from a window, at how constrained and routine our lives have become.

As we reflect, we throw off our customary and dangerous bravery, and let our sadness take its natural shape. We dwell at length on the wounds. We give space to our nostalgia. There may not be an immediate solution to the sorrows, but it helps immeasurably to know their contours and give ourselves a chance to square up to them. Our pains need a hearing. Then we give similar attention to our excitements: we stoop down to listen to their animated call. We imagine reforming our lives under their guidance. We take on board the positive, necessary anxiety that arises from admitting how many opportunities still remain to us and how much the status quo can and must be changed.

The more we think, the more our fears, resentments and hopes become easier to name. We grow less scared of the contents of our minds. We feel calmer, less resentful and clearer about our direction. We recognise how much we depend – perhaps without knowing it – on the practice of philosophy: that is, on the pursuit of accurate, clear and manageable knowledge.

2
Obstacles to Meaning

i. Vague self-understanding

We want our lives to be meaningful, but there is too often a gap between our intentions and our realities. Some of the obstacles to meaning are external (wars, financial turmoil, etc.). But there are several issues in our own minds that block access to a more meaningful existence.

We may be aware of having meaningful experiences but lack the investigative rigour to identify their origins and make-up, and therefore fail to know how to recreate them and integrate them more reliably in our lives.

We may, for example, have a particularly interesting evening with a friend. We're amazed by the conversation, wish it could happen more often and yet are at a loss as to how to engineer a more regularly satisfying social life. Or we may go on a holiday with our family, which, for once, works well, but we don't stop to examine why and the next time around, end up on a break marred by the usual litany of arguments and dissatisfactions. At work, a specific project may play to our strengths, but we're unable to decode quite why and are later moved to another department where we never again exert ourselves with comparable creativity. At home, once in a while, we find that we have a tender, playful and cathartic conversation with our partner, but can't understand in detail what might lie behind the heart-warming interlude.

Our meaningful moments threaten to be like beautiful squares in a foreign city that we stumble into at night but can never find our way back to in the light of day. We recognise their value without knowing how to rediscover them. We do not interpret them as the threads of a tapestry of meaning that we need to discover and hold onto across the labyrinth of our lives. We continue to encounter meaning a little too much by chance. We forage rather than systematically harvest.

ii. Provincialism

Another reason why we hold back from the things that yield meaning is that they can seem abnormal. We know they are valuable; we are just afraid of seeming weird by pursuing them. We may really like getting up at 3 a.m., having a long bath in the dark and thinking for hours about our childhoods. In our social lives, our real preference might be to see people for one-on-one conversations where the agenda would be abstract and announced beforehand. With our work, we know we do our best thinking in railway station cafés rather than in the cubicle where people expect us to be. On holiday, we have a yearning to visit the local sewage works and electricity plant rather than the beach or museum.

But, haunted by the fear of being abnormal, we can end up following few of our authentic inclinations. The pity is that we probably take our cue about what is normal from a specific, and not particularly representative, group of people: those who just happen to be in the vicinity. The oppressive impact of a local clan is what used to make school especially dispiriting. Fourteen-year-olds have very emphatic ideas about what counts as 'normal'. In the provincial microsociety of school, it might have been normal to think that if someone had unfashionable shoes, they should be insulted at break time; that an enthusiasm for study was contemptible, or that being a footballer represented the summit of existence. As soon as we left school, we realised that what counted as normal there wasn't normal at all. We learnt that our old classmates were, in fact, highly provincial; that is, cockily sure – but utterly wrong in thinking – that their narrow beliefs were universal markers of truth and value.

The problem with this susceptibility to provincial patterns of thinking is that it may pursue us beyond the school gates. At work, people may take it for granted that a holiday must be taken somewhere sunny: if we were to announce that we were going to spend a week in the Netherlands to admire the grey cloud banks, we might be mocked and patronised. Or there might be a powerful consensus in our social circle that, on Sundays, it is a sign of virtue to have a long lunch in company and that anyone who prefers to spend time alone writing up their journal must be distinctly odd and suspect.

But, in truth, many ideas of normality are neither universal nor incontestable. It would be wholly possible to assemble large groups of impressive people who would take quite contrary views. In the company of 17th-century Dutch landscape painters, admiring grey clouds would be a prime virtue. If we lived around Balzac, Baudelaire or Proust, our apparently eccentric preferences for lying in bed thinking on weekends would be taken for granted.

Our pursuit of a meaningful life can become fatally derailed by ideas of what is normal that are not actually normal. We should not so much abandon the notion of fitting in as imaginatively reconfigure whom we want to fit in with, and it might not be those in our immediate vicinity. We should dare to create our own imaginative communities to liberate us from the more inhibiting and asphyxiating assumptions of our neighbours.

iii. Selflessness

We are highly attuned to the notion that being selfish is one of the worst character traits we might possess, a way of behaving associated with greed, entitlement and cruelty. And yet some of the reasons we fail to have the lives we should spring from an excess of the opposite trait: an overweening modesty; an over-hasty deference to the wishes of others; a dangerous and counter-productive lack of selfishness.

We are at risk because we fail to distinguish between good and bad versions of selfishness. The good, desirable kind involves the courage to give priority to ourselves and our concerns at particular points; the confidence to be forthright about our needs, not in order to harm or conclusively reject other people, but in order to serve them in a deeper, more sustained and committed way over the long term. Bad selfishness, on the other hand, operates with no greater end in view and with no higher motive in mind. We do not decline to help so as to marshal our resources to offer others a greater gift down the line; we just can't be bothered.

Unfortunately, afflicted by confusion about this distinction, we frequently fail to state our needs as clearly as we should, with disastrous results for those we're meant to serve. In order to be a good parent, we may need to have an hour to ourselves every day. We may need to take a long time in a hot shower so as to mull over events. We may need to do something that seems a bit indulgent, like taking a life drawing class or a piano lesson. But because we sense how contrary to expectations these desires can seem, we opt to stay quiet about our requirements, and so grow increasingly ragged, angry and bitter with those who rely on us. A lack of selfishness can slowly turn us into highly disagreeable as well as ineffective people.

To take another example, we may find that our mind is at its best immediately after dinner and yet know the family tradition of spending twenty minutes tidying up the kitchen together following a meal. We accept that it would look selfish to the others to slip out at this point. We would be mocked and cast aside, so we mop the floor and scrub the potato dish and don't work out how to rearrange the cash flow in the company or practise a speech for the conference – initiatives that would, in the long term, have been of greater use to those we love than our resentful and agitated domestic efforts.

Good selfishness grows out of an accurate understanding of what we need to do in order to maximise our utility for others. It stems from an unembarrassed sense of how we should develop our abilities, get our minds into the right frame, summon up our most useful powers and organise our thoughts and feelings so that they can eventually be helpful to the world. We recognise that we will, at select moments, have to back out of doing things that people would like us to, and have no compunction about politely explaining this – unlike the selfless, who will dutifully smile, then one day explode in vindictive, exhausted rage. We know, as kind egoists, that we may be confused with the mean-spirited, but our innate conviction in our sincerity lends us the calm to pursue our aims in our own way.

The trick is to become better ambassadors of our intentions, learning persuasively to convey to those around us that we are not lazy or callous, but will simply better serve their needs by not doing the expected things for a while. We avoid becoming a nuisance to those around us by what is only ever superficially a good idea: always putting other people first.

iv. Immortality

We rightly think that fear is the enemy of the well-lived life. But there is a powerful way in which fear can play an opposite and more constructive role: it can be the psychological force that positively propels us towards a more meaningful existence.

One of the big obstacles to meaning is the feeling that we have time to get around to the important things. We recognise where the sources of meaning lie, but lack urgency in focusing on them, because we will address them tomorrow, at the end of the month, or next year. We have a hazy supposition that time is unlimited.

The horrific but inevitable fact of our own mortality is kept at bay for the most sympathetic of reasons: we can't bear the brevity of our own existence. But in so doing, we fail to give our lives the meaningful direction they deserve. We give in to localised, small-scale obstructions: the worry that something is a touch dull; the fear of looking a bit of a fool; the pain of being rejected; the awkwardness of not fitting in; the annoyance of having to make yet another effort in the same old direction. We don't persist with worthwhile things through the suffering they involve and, in the process, end up slowly ruining the time we have left.

A decisive barrier to the more meaningful lives we seek is the half-formed, secret and deeply dangerous suspicion that we may be immortal.

v. The art of storytelling

At moments of sorrow and exhaustion, it is only too easy to look back over the years and feel that our lives have, in essence, been meaningless. We take stock of just how much has gone wrong; how many errors there have been, how many unfulfilled plans and frustrated dreams we've had. We may feel like the distraught, damned Macbeth who, on learning of his wife's death, exclaims at a pitch of agony that man is a cursed creature who:

> …struts and frets his hour upon the stage,
> And then is heard no more. [Life] is a tale
> Told by an idiot, full of sound and fury,
> Signifying nothing.
>
> Shakespeare, *Macbeth*, Act 5, scene 5

No life can avoid an intermittently high degree of 'sound and fury'. The question is whether it must also, ultimately, signify nothing. As Macbeth's lines hint, this will depend on who is telling the story. In the hands of Shakespeare's bracingly termed 'idiot', the story of a life may well turn into unintelligible and dispiriting gibberish. But with sufficient compassion and insight, we may be able to make something different and a great deal more meaningful and redemptive out of the same material.

Only a small number of people ever self-consciously write their autobiographies. It is a task we associate with celebrities and the very old, but it is, in the background, a universal activity. We may not be publishing our stories, but we are writing them in our minds nevertheless. Every day finds us weaving a story about who we are, where we are going, and why events happened as they did.

Many of us are strikingly harsh narrators of these life stories. We declare our achievements puny; we berate ourselves for our faults; we perceive only the negative sides of our characters. We constantly give the advantage to the other side. We may feel that we're being objective, but it seems we are really rehearsing the case for an especially vicious imaginary prosecution.

Yet there is nothing necessary about our methods or our verdicts. There could be ways of telling very different, far kinder and more balanced stories from the same sets of facts. Good narrators – ones who are fair-minded and judicious – know how to display a range of narrative skills that keep unfair, partisan and confidence-destroying lines of attack at bay. These good narrators accept that lives can be meaningful even when they involve a lot of failure and humiliation. Mistakes are not dead ends; they are sources of information that can be exploited and put to work as guides to more effective subsequent action. The sound and fury can be made to yield hugely significant insights.

The good storyteller appreciates that a life can remain meaningful even when it contains long passages that might appear, at first glance, to be merely a waste of time. We may spend a decade not knowing what we want to do professionally, trying out different jobs and never settling in any of them, testing our parents and enduring the scepticism of our friends. We may go through a succession of failed relationships that leave us confused and hurt. But these experiences don't have to be dismissed as meaningless. The wandering and the exploration may be intimately connected to our eventual development and growth. We needed the career crisis to understand our working identities; we had to fail at love to fathom our hearts. We cannot get anywhere important in one go. We must forgive ourselves the horrors of our first drafts.

The good storyteller recognises too, contrary to certain impressions, that there will always be a number of players responsible for negative events in a person's life. We are never the sole authors of our triumphs or of our defeats. It is therefore as unwarranted (and as egocentric) to take all the blame as to assume all the credit. Sometimes, it really will be the fault of something or somebody else: the economy, our parents, the government, our enemies, or sheer bad luck. We should not take the entire burden of our difficulties upon our own shoulders.

Good narrators are compassionate. At many points, we simply could not have known. We were not exceptionally stupid, we were – like all humans – operating with limited information, trying to interpret the world with flawed and blinkered minds under the constant sway of emotion, damaged by our pasts and only selectively capable of reason and calm.

Finally, good narrators appreciate that events can count as meaningful even when they aren't recognised as such by powerful authorities in the world at large. We may be holidaying in a tent rather than in the Presidential suite, hanging out with our grandmother rather than a pop group, teaching children to read rather than buying and selling companies, and nevertheless lay claim to a legitimately meaningful life. We should not let false notions of prestige interfere with our attempts to focus on the aspects of our life stories that actually satisfy us.

On our death beds, we will inevitably know that much didn't work out; that there were dreams that didn't come to pass and loves that were rejected; friendships that could never be repaired, and catastrophes and hurts we never overcame. But we will also know that there were threads of value that sustained us, that there was a higher logic we sometimes followed, that despite the agonies, our lives were not mere sound and fury; that in our own way, at select moments at least, we did properly draw benefit from, and understand, the meaning of life.

Picture credits

Cover	Jill Ferry / Getty Images
p. 22	Titian, *Pope Paul III and His Grandsons*, 1545–1546. Bridgeman Images
p. 40	Paul Cézanne, *Montagne Sainte-Victoire with a Large Pine*, c. 1887. Oil on canvas, 66.8 × 92.3 cm. Photo © The Courtauld / Bridgeman Images
p. 43	Hojo-Teien (Garden of the Abbot's Hall) comprised of rock, moss and gravel at Tofuku-ji temple, Kyoto, Japan. Judy Bellah / Alamy Stock Photo
p. 47	Pablo Picasso, *Tête de Taureau (Bull's Head)*, 1942. Bicycle seat and handlebars, 33.5 × 43.5 × 19 cm. Musée Picasso, Paris © Succession Picasso / DACS, London 2024
p. 65	View of the Temple of Athena Nike, Acropolis of Athens. © Antonio Amato / Dreamstime.com
p. 67 (left)	Armchair made for Morris & Co. c. 1864–1865 (stained ash with rush seat), probably designed by Ford Madox Brown (1821–1893) after chairs from Sussex. Collection The Cheltenham Trust and Cheltenham Borough Council. Photo © The Wilson / Bridgeman Images
p. 67 (right)	Le Corbusier, Pierre Jeanneret and Charlotte Perriand, *Fauteuil B 301*, 1928. Paris, Centre Pompidou – Musée national d'art moderne – Centre de création industrielle . ADAGP, Paris and DACS, London / FLC / ADAGP, Paris and DACS, London 2024
p. 79	Peter Blake, *Self-Portrait with Badges*, 1961. Oil paint on board, frame: 1792 × 1265 × 70 mm. Tate, London © Peter Blake 2018. All rights reserved, DACS 2024

p. 92   The Discobolus Lancellotti, Roman copy in marble of a 5th-century BCE Greek original by Myron, Hadrianic period. Palazzo Massimo alle Terme, Rome. Photo: Carole Raddato / followinghadrian.com

Also available from The School of Life:

The School of Life: Calm
The harmony and serenity we crave

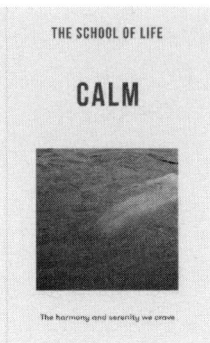

A guide to developing the art of finding serenity by understanding the sources of our anxiety and frustrations.

Few life skills are as neglected, yet as important, as the ability to remain calm. Our very worst decisions and interactions are almost invariably the result of a loss of calm – and a descent into anxiety and agitation.

Surprisingly, but very fortunately, our power to remain calm can be rehearsed and improved. We don't have to stay where we are now: our responses to everyday challenges can dramatically alter. We can educate ourselves in the art of keeping calm not through slow breathing or special teas but through thinking. This is a book that patiently unpacks the causes of our greatest stresses and gives us a succession of highly persuasive, beautiful and sometimes dryly comic arguments with which to defend ourselves against panic and fury.

UK ISBN: 978-1-912891-98-6 / US ISBN: 978-1-915087-14-0

The School of Life: Small Pleasures
What makes life truly valuable

Explores and appreciates the small pleasures found in everyday life.

So often, we exhaust ourselves and the planet in a search for very large pleasures, while all around us lies a wealth of small pleasures, which – if only we paid more attention – could daily bring us solace and joy at little cost and effort. But we need some encouragement to focus our gaze.

This is a book to guide us to the best of life's small pleasures: everything from the distinctive delight of holding a child's hand to the enjoyment of disagreeing with someone or the joy of the evening sky; an intriguing, evocative mix of small pleasures that will heighten our senses and return us to the world with new-found excitement and enthusiasm.

UK ISBN: 978-1-915087-03-4 / US ISBN: 978-1-915087-16-4

The School of Life: A Job to Love
How to find a fulfilling career

A practical guide to finding fulfilling work by understanding yourself.

Alongside a satisfying relationship, a career we love is one of the most important requirements for a fulfilled life. Unfortunately, it is devilishly hard to understand oneself well enough to know quite where one's energies should be directed.

It is to help us out of some of these impasses that we wrote *A Job to Love*, a guide to how we can better understand ourselves and locate a job that is right for us. With compassion and a deeply practical spirit, the book guides us to discover our true talents and to make sense of our confused desires and aspirations before it is too late.

UK ISBN: 978-1-915087-06-5 / US ISBN: 978-1-915087-31-7

The School of Life: On Being Nice
A guide to friendship and connection

A guide to rediscovering niceness as one of the highest of all human achievements.

Most books that want to change us seek to make us richer or thinner. This book wants to help us to be nicer: that is, less irritable, more patient, readier to listen, warmer, less prickly ... Niceness may not have the immediate allure of money or fame, but it is a hugely important quality nevertheless and one that we neglect at our peril.

This is a guide to the uncharted landscape of niceness, gently leading us around the key themes of this forgotten quality. We learn how to be charitable, how to forgive, how to be natural and how to reassure. We learn that niceness is compatible with strength and is no indicator of naivety. Niceness deserves to be rediscovered as one of the highest of all human achievements.

UK ISBN: 978-1-915087-02-7 / US ISBN: 978-1-915087-15-7

How to Travel

A philosophical guide to fulfilling journeys

A guide to how we can travel better, so that our experiences overseas become transformative and memorable.

Going travelling is one of the few things we undertake in a direct attempt to make ourselves happy – and frequently, in fascinating ways, we fail. We get bored, cross, anxious or lonely. It isn't surprising: our societies act as if going travelling were simple, just a case of handing over the right sum of money. But a satisfying journey isn't something we can simply buy; it's the result of an art that has to be learnt.

This is the guide: not to any one destination but to travel in general. It talks to us, among other things, about how we should choose a place to go, what we might do when we get there and how we should make good moments stick in our minds. In a succession of genial essays, we become students of an unexpected but vital topic: how to understand and more fully enjoy (what should be) some of the finest experiences of our lives.

ISBN: 978-1-9999179-6-8

Reasons to be Hopeful

What remains consoling, inspiring and beautiful

An honest and accessible guide to finding light in the darkest of times.

In a world that isn't short of darkness, there can be few more urgent priorities than to spend time rehearsing for ourselves why life – despite all its challenges – still has so much to offer us; why there are still so many reasons to be hopeful.

Here is a collection of some of the most persuasive arguments for staying on the side of optimism, creativity, kindness, calm and hope. Across a series of essays, we learn why we still have the right to feel purposeful and buoyant despite everything that is challenging.

The book urges us to reconnect with our more resilient selves, bidding us to recover faith in what is still possible. At points funny and always encouraging and kind, here is an ideal friend to guide us back to courage and delight.

ISBN: 978-1-912891-89-4

Philosophy in 40 Ideas
Lessons for life

A thought-provoking introduction to philosophy; spanning the history of thought in 40 key ideas.

Philosophy is a practical discipline committed to helping us live wiser and less sorrowful lives. This book draws together 40 of the greatest ideas found in Eastern and Western philosophy, spanning the history of thought from Socrates to the Buddha, Jean-Paul Sartre to Lao Tzu. We are reminded of the wit, humanity and relevance of the great thinkers, who have hugely helpful things to say to us about falling in love, making friends, finding serenity, discovering our purpose and enjoying what remains of our lives.

Here are the most essential ideas from philosophy rescued, highlighted and inspiringly presented so they can help where they are most needed: in our daily lives.

ISBN: 978-1-912891-47-4

To join The School of Life community and find out more, scan below:

The School of Life publishes a range of books on essential topics in psychological and emotional life, including relationships, parenting, friendship, careers and fulfilment. The aim is always to help us to understand ourselves better and thereby to grow calmer, less confused and more purposeful. Discover our full range of titles, including books for children, here:
www.theschooloflife.com/books

The School of Life also offers a comprehensive therapy service, which complements, and draws upon, our published works:
www.theschooloflife.com/therapy

THESCHOOLOFLIFE.COM

Varieties of Melancholy
A hopeful guide to our sombre moods

An insightful and consoling guide to the melancholic state of mind.

This is a book that celebrates the most neglected but valuable emotion we can feel: melancholy. Melancholy isn't depression, rage or bitterness; it's a serene, wise and kindly response to the difficulties of being alive. It steers a midway course between despair on the one hand and naïve optimism on the other. But melancholy is a well-kept secret. We don't often hear melancholy being celebrated or accorded the respect that it deserves. It languishes unexplored in a hypercompetitive, noisy and frantic age.

Offering a varied portrait of melancholy and its range of manifestations, *Varieties of Melancholy* leads the reader to insight, acceptance and self-compassion.

ISBN: 978-1-912891-60-3